PROCRASTINATION

DETOX

A 21-DAY ACTION PLAN FOR A PRODUCTIVE LIFE

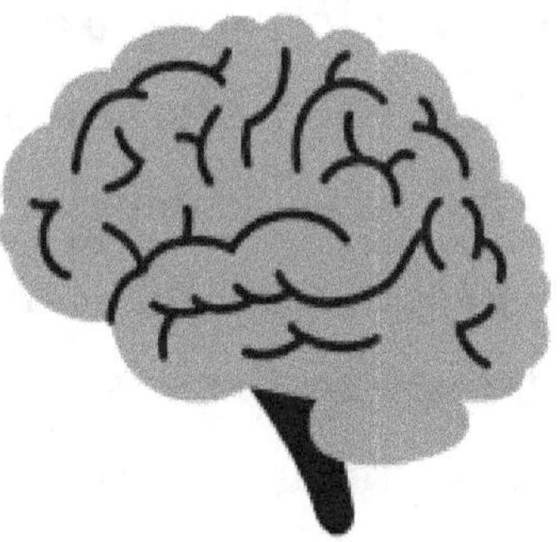

Jeffrey Ani

Procrastination Detox: A 21-Day Action Plan for a Productive Life

Copyright © 2023 by Jeffrey Ani

TABLE OF CONTENTS

INTRODUCTION

Welcome to Procrastination Detox: A 21-Day Action Plan for a Productive Life! Are you tired of constantly putting off important tasks, feeling overwhelmed by the weight of unfinished projects, and wondering why you can't seem to break free from the chains of procrastination? If that's the case, you've arrived at the right place.

The importance of addressing procrastination

In this book, we'll embark on a transformative journey together—a journey that will help you detox your mind, boost your motivation, and ignite your productivity. Over the next 21 days, you'll engage in a series of daily exercises, delve into inspiring stories, and learn proven techniques to finally conquer procrastination and reclaim control of your life.

But before we dive into the program, let's take a moment to understand why addressing procrastination is crucial and how this 21-day detox can be the catalyst for real change.

Procrastination has a way of creeping into every aspect of our lives. It silently sabotages our goals, dreams, and potential. It disguises itself as comfort, as the temporary relief from the anxiety of starting something new or facing a difficult task. Yet, as the days turn into weeks, and weeks into months, we find ourselves buried under a mountain of unfinished business, feeling frustrated, unfulfilled, and stuck in a cycle of inaction.

How the 21-day program works

But fear not! This book is your roadmap to freedom. It will equip you with the tools, strategies, and mindset shifts necessary to break free from the grip of procrastination. The 21-day program is designed to be both a challenge and a support system. It will push you out of your comfort zone while providing you with the guidance and encouragement you need to succeed.

Setting realistic expectations

Now, let's set some expectations. Overcoming procrastination is not an overnight process. It requires dedication, perseverance, and a commitment to change. While the 21-day program is intensive, it serves as a launching pad for your ongoing journey towards a more productive life.

Throughout this book, you'll gain insights into the psychology behind procrastination, explore common triggers, and uncover the deeper reasons why you've been putting things off. You'll also discover practical techniques to boost your motivation, create an environment conducive to productivity, and develop effective time management skills.

But remember, this is not a one-size-fits-all solution. Each person's journey is unique, and it's essential to approach this program with an open mind, ready to adapt the strategies to your own circumstances. Embrace the process, even if it feels uncomfortable or challenging at times, because on the other side lies the liberating joy of getting things done and achieving your goals.

Are you ready to take the leap? Are you ready to break free from the chains of procrastination and embark on a 21-day adventure that will transform your habits and unlock your true potential? If your answer is a resounding "yes," then let's dive in and begin our Procrastination Detox together. Get ready to unleash the power within you and discover a life of productivity, fulfillment, and accomplishment. The time for action is now!

CHAPTER 1: UNDERSTANDING PROCRASTINATION

Understanding Procrastination

Congratulations on embarking on this transformative journey! In this chapter, we will dive deep into the murky waters of procrastination and explore its impact on our productivity and overall well-being. Get ready to unravel the tangled web of procrastination and gain a deeper understanding of its underlying mechanisms.

Procrastination is a sneaky little devil that loves to wreak havoc on our lives. It manifests itself in various ways, disguising laziness as relaxation and time-wasting as "me time." We often find ourselves falling victim to its seductive allure, only to wake up one day surrounded by a pile of unfinished tasks, deadlines looming ominously overhead.

But fear not! By gaining a clearer understanding of procrastination, we can begin to dismantle its hold on us. So, let's strip away the layers and get to the core of this perplexing phenomenon.

Defining procrastination and its impact on productivity

At its core, procrastination is a coping mechanism—a way for us to deal with the uncomfortable emotions and uncertainties that come with starting or completing a task. It's like a security blanket that shields us from the fear of failure, the fear of judgment, and the fear of stepping out of our comfort zones.

But here's the perplexing part: while procrastination provides temporary relief, it ultimately sabotages our long-term goals and aspirations. It creates a vicious cycle of stress, guilt, and self-doubt. We find ourselves caught in a never-ending loop of delaying, rationalizing, and promising to do better tomorrow.

Recognizing common triggers and behaviors

To truly break free from this cycle, we must examine the triggers and behaviors that perpetuate our procrastination habits. Is it the fear of making mistakes? The overwhelming magnitude of a task? Or perhaps it's the allure of instant gratification and the temptation to indulge in mindless distractions.

By shining a light on these triggers, we can gain insight into our own patterns of procrastination. Awareness is the first step towards change, and as we embark on this 21-day journey, we will explore our procrastination traps, peel back the layers of our habits, and discover the reasons behind our tendencies to delay.

Exploring the costs and consequences of procrastination

But why is it so important to address procrastination? The answer lies in the consequences it brings. Procrastination robs us of precious time, energy, and opportunities. It prevents us from reaching our full potential and living the fulfilling lives we desire. It hampers our personal and professional growth, leaving us feeling stagnant and unfulfilled.

Imagine a life where you no longer feel burdened by unfinished tasks and looming deadlines. Imagine the freedom and liberation that come with taking decisive action and crossing off items on your to-do list with confidence and ease. That is the promise of conquering procrastination.

As we move forward in this book, remember that change is possible. You have already taken the first step by acknowledging the need for transformation.

In the next chapter, we will delve into the process of preparing for the procrastination detox. We will assess our current habits, set meaningful goals, and create a supportive environment that will set us up for success. Get ready to take charge of your life and break free from the chains of procrastination. The journey has just begun!

CHAPTER 2: PREPARING FOR THE DETOX

Welcome to the second chapter of our exhilarating journey towards a procrastination-free existence! In this chapter, we will lay the groundwork for your ultimate success by preparing for the procrastination detox. Get ready to roll up your sleeves, challenge your preconceptions, and embark on a transformative adventure!

Assessing your current habits and patterns

Before we dive into the nitty-gritty details, take a moment to reflect on your current habits and patterns. What are the behaviors that have led you down the treacherous path of procrastination? Are there specific triggers that consistently derail your progress? Understanding your starting point is crucial for charting a new course.

Setting meaningful goals for the program

Now, it's time to set meaningful goals that will guide you throughout this 21-day program. Keep in mind that goals ought to be clear, quantifiable, reachable, pertinent, and time-bound. Think about what you truly want to achieve and how conquering procrastination will bring you closer to those aspirations.

But beware! Resistance and fear may rear their ugly heads as you embark on this journey. The comfort of familiarity can be seductive, and your mind may attempt to convince you that change is unnecessary or impossible. This is where your determination and commitment to growth come into play.

Challenge those limiting beliefs and embrace the discomfort of stepping out of your comfort zone. Remember, the magic happens outside of your comfort zone, where possibilities and personal growth await.

Creating a supportive environment

Creating a supportive environment is crucial to your success. Surround yourself with people who uplift and motivate you. Share your goals with them, and let their positive energy propel you forward. Additionally, consider decluttering your physical and digital spaces to eliminate distractions and create an environment conducive to focus and productivity.

Overcoming fear and resistance to change

Now, let's address the elephant in the room: fear. Fear of failure, fear of judgment, fear of the unknown—they can all paralyze us and keep us trapped in the clutches of procrastination. But here's the secret: fear is merely a figment of our imagination, a creation of our minds.

It's time to reframe your relationship with fear. See it as a sign that you are pushing yourself beyond your comfort zone, a signal that you are on the brink of growth and transformation. Embrace the unknown, for it is in the uncertainty that you will discover your true potential.

As you embark on this 21-day program, remember that you are not alone. Countless individuals have embarked on this journey before you, overcoming their own procrastination demons and emerging victorious. Their stories of triumph and resilience serve as beacons of hope and inspiration.

Now, take a deep breath and let go of any doubts or hesitations that may linger. The journey ahead will test your resolve, challenge your assumptions, and ignite the fire of transformation within you.

In the next chapter, we will dive into Day 1 of our procrastination detox: building awareness. Brace yourself for a powerful exploration of your own procrastination patterns, as we unravel the mysteries of your habits and begin the process of change. Get ready to confront the demons head-on and emerge stronger than ever before. The time for action is now!

CHAPTER 3: DAY 1 - BUILDING AWARENESS

Welcome to Day 1 of our exhilarating journey towards overcoming procrastination! Today, we dive headfirst into building awareness—the foundation upon which our transformation will be built. Prepare to unravel the intricacies of your procrastination patterns and gain a deeper understanding of the traps that have held you back.

Reflecting on Your Procrastination Patterns

Take a moment to reflect on your past experiences with procrastination. What tasks or projects have you consistently put off? Are there specific circumstances or triggers that lead to procrastination? Reflecting on your patterns is the first step toward understanding the intricacies of your procrastination habits.

As you engage in this reflection, be prepared to face the truth with honesty and curiosity. Don't judge yourself harshly for past procrastination blunders.

Instead, view them as valuable learning experiences that can guide you toward growth and change.

Identifying Your Most Common Procrastination Traps

Now that you've reflected on your procrastination patterns, it's time to identify your most common traps. These traps can be internal or external factors that contribute to your tendency to delay tasks. They might include perfectionism, fear of failure, lack of clear goals, or even excessive reliance on digital distractions.

By identifying your specific procrastination traps, you'll gain insight into the underlying causes of your procrastination. Remember, each person's traps may be unique, so take the time to explore your own tendencies fully.

Developing Self-Awareness through Journaling

Journaling is a powerful tool for developing self-awareness. It allows you to dive deep into your thoughts and emotions, helping you uncover patterns and triggers that contribute to procrastination. Set aside some dedicated time each day to journal about your experiences, feelings, and observations related to procrastination.

As you journal, explore questions such as: What emotions arise when faced with a task? Are there recurring thought patterns that accompany your procrastination? How does procrastination affect your mood and overall well-being? By delving into these questions, you'll gain a clearer understanding of the internal dynamics that drive your procrastination habits.

Cultivating Mindfulness as a Tool for Change

Mindfulness is an essential tool in our journey towards overcoming procrastination. By cultivating mindfulness, we learn to observe our thoughts and emotions without judgment or attachment. It allows us to recognize the moment when we begin to slide into the familiar territory of procrastination.

Practice incorporating mindfulness into your daily routine. Meditation, deep breathing exercises, and mindful walking are some activities you can explore. By staying present in the moment, you can catch yourself when you start to veer off track and redirect your focus towards productive action.

Remember, building awareness is an ongoing process. As you move forward in this 21-day program, continue to reflect, identify traps, journal, and cultivate mindfulness. This journey may challenge you at times, but rest assured that each step brings you closer to breaking free from the chains of procrastination.

In the next chapter, we'll delve into Days 2 to 7, where we'll explore mindset shifts and techniques to boost your motivation. Get ready for a burst of inspiration and empowerment as we propel ourselves further along this transformative path. The adventure continues, and the promise of a more productive life beckons. Embrace the journey and prepare for the revelations that lie ahead!

CHAPTER 4: DAY 2-7 - MINDSET SHIFT

Welcome to Days 2-7 of the Procrastination Detox! In this chapter, we will dive deep into the realm of mindset, exploring the power of our thoughts, beliefs, and self-talk. Get ready to uncover the limiting beliefs that hold you back, challenge negative thought patterns, and cultivate a growth mindset that will propel you towards productivity and success.

Uncovering Limiting Beliefs and Self-Talk

Limiting beliefs are like invisible barriers that hinder our progress and keep us trapped in a cycle of procrastination. They are often the result of past experiences, societal conditioning or fear of failure. You need to consider the beliefs and abilities you hold about yourself for a while.

What stories do you tell yourself? Are there recurring negative self-talk patterns that undermine your confidence and motivation? By shining a light on these beliefs and self-talk, you can start to challenge their validity and replace them with more empowering narratives.

Challenging Negative Thought Patterns

Negative thought patterns can be relentless, feeding into our doubts and reinforcing our procrastination habits. It's time to break free from this destructive cycle. When you catch yourself engaging in negative self-talk or entertaining thoughts of self-doubt, take a step back and challenge their accuracy.

Ask yourself: Are these thoughts based on evidence or assumptions? Are there alternative perspectives that could be more empowering and supportive? By challenging negative thought patterns, you can

reframe your mindset and cultivate a more positive
and productive outlook.

Cultivating a Growth Mindset

A growth mindset is the belief that our abilities and
intelligence can be developed through effort, practice,
and perseverance. It's the belief that we can learn
from failure, embrace challenges, and continuously
improve. Cultivating a growth mindset is a powerful
tool for overcoming procrastination.

Embrace the idea that mistakes and setbacks are
opportunities for growth and learning. Emphasize the
process rather than solely focusing on the end result.
Embrace challenges as chances to stretch your
abilities and expand your comfort zone. By adopting a
growth mindset, you'll approach tasks with
enthusiasm and resilience, ready to tackle them head-
on.

Practicing Positive Affirmations and Visualization

Positive affirmations and visualization are powerful
techniques for reprogramming your mind and

reinforcing positive beliefs. Affirmations are positive declarations that you repeat to yourself to help you maintain a positive mindset. Visualization involves creating vivid mental images of yourself successfully completing tasks and achieving your goals.

Integrate positive affirmations into your daily routine, repeating them regularly to counteract negative self-talk. Visualize yourself taking action, being productive, and accomplishing your goals. Allow these mental images to fuel your motivation and inspire you to take consistent steps towards your desired outcomes.

As Days 2-7 of the Procrastination Detox come to an end, celebrate the progress you've made in shifting your mindset. Remember, a positive and empowering mindset is the cornerstone of productivity.

In the next chapter, we will delve into Days 8-14, where we'll focus on developing effective time management skills and creating a structured routine that supports your productivity. Get ready to optimize your time and unleash your potential. The adventure continues, and you're on your way to a more productive life!

CHAPTER 5: DAY 8-14 MOTIVATION BOOST

Welcome to Days 8-14 of the Procrastination Detox! In this chapter, we will dive deep into the realm of motivation, exploring the factors that drive us to take action and stay focused on our goals. Get ready to explore intrinsic and extrinsic motivation, discover your personal values and goals, create a compelling vision for your future, and cultivate motivation through rewards and accountability.

Exploring Intrinsic and Extrinsic Motivation

Motivation can stem from both intrinsic and extrinsic sources. Intrinsic motivation comes from within and is driven by personal satisfaction, enjoyment, or a sense of purpose. Extrinsic motivation, on the other hand, arises from external rewards or consequences. Reflect on the factors that motivate you and consider how both intrinsic and extrinsic motivations play a role in your life.

Understanding what drives you will help you harness your motivation more effectively. It allows you to align your goals and tasks with your values and interests, creating a stronger sense of purpose and fulfillment.

Discovering Your Personal Values and Goals

To stay motivated, it's important to have clarity about your personal values and goals. Take some time to consider what is truly important to you in life. What are your core values, those guiding principles that shape your decisions and actions? What are your short-term and long-term goals, both personal and professional?

Identifying your values and goals provides a compass to navigate through life. It allows you to prioritize tasks and make choices that align with your vision of a fulfilling and purposeful life. Embrace this process of self-discovery as you uncover your deepest aspirations and desires.

Creating a Compelling Vision for Your Future

A compelling vision acts as a beacon that guides your actions and fuels your motivation. Envision your ideal future, the life you desire to create for yourself. What does it look like? How does it feel? Paint a vivid picture in your mind and let it inspire you.

By creating a compelling vision, you tap into the power of your imagination and connect with your inner drive. It becomes a source of inspiration and motivation, propelling you forward even when faced with challenges. Embrace the perplexity of envisioning a future that excites and energizes you.

Cultivating Motivation through Rewards and Accountability

Rewards and accountability can be powerful tools to boost motivation and keep you on track. Consider implementing a reward system where you celebrate small milestones and achievements along the way.

These rewards can be as simple as treating yourself to something you enjoy or taking a well-deserved break.

Additionally, accountability plays a crucial role in maintaining motivation. Share your objectives and progress with a trustworthy friend, family member, or mentor who can offer encouragement and hold you accountable. Regular check-ins and progress updates can keep you motivated and committed to your journey.

As Days 8-14 of the Procrastination Detox come to an end, celebrate the progress you've made in boosting your motivation. Remember, motivation is the fuel that propels you towards your goals. I urge you to embrace this transformative journey as we move forward to explore more strategies and techniques in the chapters to come.

In the next chapter, we will delve into Days 15-21, where we'll focus on overcoming obstacles and developing resilience in the face of challenges. Get ready to overcome setbacks and emerge stronger than ever. The adventure continues, and your productivity journey is reaching new heights!

CHAPTER 6: DAY 15-21 ACTION AND PRODUCTIVITY

Welcome to Days 15-21 of the Procrastination Detox! In this chapter, we will focus on taking action and boosting your productivity. It's time to put all the knowledge and insights you've gained into practice. Get ready to develop effective time management strategies, break tasks into manageable steps, create a compelling vision for your future, and harness the power of focus and concentration.

Developing Effective Time Management Strategies

Time management is essential for maximizing productivity and achieving your goals. Reflect on how you currently manage your time and identify areas for improvement. Consider using techniques such as prioritization, scheduling, and creating to-do lists.

Explore different time management methods and find what works best for you. Whether it's the Pomodoro Technique, time blocking, or using productivity apps, experiment with various strategies to optimize your time and make the most of each day.

Breaking Tasks into Manageable Steps

One of the biggest challenges when faced with a daunting task is knowing where to start. Breaking tasks into manageable steps makes them more approachable and less overwhelming. Begin by identifying the main objective and then break it down into smaller, actionable tasks.

By breaking tasks into manageable steps, you create a clear roadmap that guides your actions. This approach enhances your productivity and provides a sense of progress as you complete each step. Try tackling one small task at a time and watch your accomplishments grow.

Creating a Compelling Vision for Your Future

A compelling vision acts as a powerful motivator for action. Revisit the vision you created earlier in this journey and bring it to life. Reflect on the impact of your actions and the fulfillment you'll experience as you move closer to your desired future.

Keep your vision at the forefront of your mind as you take action. Let it inspire you to stay focused and committed. Allow the congruency between your vision and your actions to guide you towards the productive life you envision for yourself.

Harnessing the Power of Focus and Concentration

In a world filled with distractions, developing the ability to focus and concentrate is crucial for productivity. Minimize external distractions by creating a conducive work environment, turning off notifications, and setting boundaries.

Practice mindfulness and engage in activities that enhance your focus, such as meditation or deep work sessions. Train your mind to stay present and fully immerse yourself in the task at hand. Embrace the perplexity of maintaining focus in a world of constant stimuli.

As Days 15-21 of the Procrastination Detox come to an end, celebrate the progress you've made in taking action and boosting your productivity. Remember, consistent action is the key to achieving your goals.

In the final chapter, we will wrap up the 21-day program, reflecting on your transformation, and providing guidance for maintaining your newfound productivity in the long run. The adventure is nearing its conclusion, and your productivity revolution is within reach!

CHAPTER 7: MAINTAINING MOMENTUM

Welcome to the final chapter of the Procrastination Detox! In this chapter, we will focus on maintaining the momentum you've built throughout the 21-day program. It's time to solidify your progress and ensure that your newfound productivity becomes a sustainable part of your life. Get ready to celebrate progress and small wins, build resilience in the face of setbacks, develop a long-term plan for productivity, and create habits to prevent relapse into procrastination.

Celebrating Progress and Small Wins

Celebrating your progress and small wins is essential for maintaining motivation and momentum. Take the time to acknowledge and appreciate how far you've come on this journey. Reflect on the milestones you've achieved, no matter how small they may seem.

By celebrating progress and small wins, you reinforce the positive habits and behaviors you've developed. Enjoy the feeling of joy and pride as you recognize the steps you've taken towards a more productive life.

Building Resilience in the Face of Setbacks

Setbacks are a natural part of any journey, including the path to overcoming procrastination. Building resilience is crucial for navigating and overcoming these obstacles. Embrace the perplexity of setbacks as opportunities for growth and learning.

When faced with a setback, practice self-compassion and remind yourself that it's a temporary detour, not a dead-end. Learn from the experience, adapt your approach if necessary, and keep moving forward. Develop a mindset that embraces challenges as opportunities to become stronger and more resilient.

Developing a Long-Term Plan for Productivity

To maintain momentum beyond the 21-day program, it's important to develop a long-term plan for productivity. Reflect on your goals and values, and consider how you can integrate productive habits into your daily life.

Identify the strategies and techniques from the Procrastination Detox that resonated most with you. Create a roadmap that outlines the actions you will take to maintain your productivity. Set realistic and achievable goals, and break them down into actionable steps.

Creating Habits to Prevent Relapse into Procrastination

Creating habits is key to preventing relapse into procrastination. Habits automate actions, making it easier to stay on track. Reflect on the habits you want to establish and consider how you can integrate them into your routine.

Start small and focus on consistency. Gradually build up your habits, making them a natural part of your day-to-day life. Embrace the congruency of aligning your habits with your values and goals, ensuring that they support your long-term productivity.

As the Procrastination Detox concludes, take a moment to reflect on your transformation and the impact it has had on your life. Remember that maintaining momentum requires ongoing effort and commitment, but the rewards are well worth it.

Congratulations on completing the Procrastination Detox! You have the tools, strategies, and mindset to lead a more productive and fulfilling life. Embrace the journey ahead, and may your productivity revolution continue to thrive.

CHAPTER 8: CONCLUSION

Reflection on the 21-day Journey

As we come to the end of the 21-day Procrastination Detox, take a moment to reflect on the journey you've embarked upon. Recall the challenges you faced, the insights you gained, and the actions you took to overcome procrastination. Consider how far you've come since the beginning and acknowledge the progress you've made.

Reflect on the lessons learned, the techniques you found most effective, and the mindset shifts that have shaped your productivity journey. Savor the accomplishment of this moment, as you realize the impact of your commitment and dedication.

Acknowledging the Transformation and Growth Achieved

It's important to acknowledge and celebrate the transformation and growth you've experienced throughout the Procrastination Detox. Recognize the positive changes in your habits, mindset, and productivity. Embrace the congruency of aligning your actions with your goals and values.

Take pride in the small and large victories you've achieved along the way. Acknowledge the perseverance and resilience you've demonstrated in overcoming challenges and setbacks. Embrace the perplexity of personal growth, as you continue to evolve and thrive.

Encouragement to Continue Practicing the Strategies

The journey towards a productive life is an ongoing process. The strategies and techniques you've learned during the 21-day program are meant to be practiced consistently. Encourage yourself to continue implementing these strategies in your daily life.

Remind yourself of the benefits you've experienced as a result of your efforts. Reap the benefits of determination and commitment, as you choose to prioritize your goals and take consistent action towards them. Remember that every small step counts and builds the foundation for long-term success.

Final Words of Inspiration and Empowerment

As you conclude the Procrastination Detox, I leave you with final words of inspiration and empowerment. You have the power to shape your life and define your productivity. Embrace the journey ahead with a sense of excitement and possibility.

Stay connected to your vision, values, and goals. Embrace the congruency of aligning your actions with your aspirations. Embrace the perplexity of challenges as opportunities for growth.

Believe in your abilities to conquer challenges. Trust in the process and the progress you've made. Remember that productivity is not just about getting things done; it's about creating a fulfilling and purposeful life.

Congratulations on completing the Procrastination Detox! You are now equipped with the tools, mindset, and strategies to lead a more productive and rewarding life. Embrace the lessons learned, the growth achieved, and continue to evolve on your journey. May you thrive in your pursuit of productivity and experience the joy of living a purposeful life.

APPENDIX

In this appendix, you will find additional resources, recommended books, apps, and tools for productivity, as well as worksheets and templates to support your 21-day Procrastination Detox program. These resources are designed to further enhance your knowledge, provide ongoing support, and help you maintain your productivity momentum.

RECOMMENDED APPS AND TOOLS

Todoist - A powerful task management app that helps you stay organized and focused.

Trello - A visual project management tool that allows you track tasks and collaborate with others.

Forest - An app that helps you stay focused and avoid distractions by growing virtual trees.

Pomodoro Technique Timer - A simple timer app that follows the Pomodoro Technique for improved focus and productivity.

Evernote - A note-taking app that allows you capture ideas, make lists, and stay organized across devices.

WORKSHEETS AND TEMPLATES

Goal Setting Worksheet - Use this worksheet to define your goals and create a clear roadmap for achieving them.

Daily Planner Template - Plan your days effectively by using this template to prioritize tasks and allocate time for important activities.

Habit Tracker - Track your progress and build new productive habits with this template.

Reflection Journal - Use this journal template to reflect on your daily achievements, challenges, and insights.

These additional resources, apps, and tools, along with the worksheets and templates, will support you in continuing your journey towards a productive life beyond the 21-day Procrastination Detox program. Feel free to explore these resources at your own pace and adapt them to your specific needs and preferences.

Remember, the key to long-term success is consistency, commitment, and ongoing growth. Embrace the knowledge and tools available to you, and continue to cultivate a mindset of productivity and fulfillment. May your journey be filled with continuous progress and joy as you create the life you desire.

Note: The worksheets, templates, and additional resources mentioned in this appendix are available for FREE download on our Gumroad page: https://inspiredman.gumroad.com

Wishing you all the best on your path to a productive and purposeful life!